The B Poems

Also by Simon Perchik

Almost Rain
St. Paul, MN: River Otter Press, 2013

Simon Perchik: Greatest Hits 1964 – 2008
Columbus, OH: Pudding House Publications, 2009

Rafts
Richmond Hill, Ontario, Canada: Parsifal Press, 2007

Hands Collected: The Books of Simon Perchik: Poems, 1949 – 1999, edited by David Baratier
Columbus, OH: Pavement Saw Press, 2000, 2003

The Autochthon Poems, introduction by Edward Butscher
Santa Monica, CA: Split Shift, 2001

Touching the Headstone
Exeter, Devon, England: Stride Publications, 2000

These Hands Filled with Numbness
Gallup, NM: Dusty Dog Press, 1996

Fourteen New Poems
Plymouth, Devon, England: Shearsman Books, 1994

The Emptiness Between My Hands
Gallup, NM: Dusty Dog Press, 1993

Letters to the Dead
Laurinburg, NC: St. Andrews College Press, 1993

Birthmark
New York City, NY: Flockophobic Press, 1992

Redeeming the Wings
Zuni, NM: Dusty Dog Press, 1991

The Gandolf Poems
Fredonia, NY: White Pine Press, 1988

Who Can Touch These Knots: New & Selected Poems
Metuchen, NJ: Scarecrow Press, 1985

The Snowcat Poems, 1980 – 1981, to the Photographs of Robert Frank
North Charleston, SC: Linwood Publishers, 1984

Mr. Lucky: Poems
Plymouth, Devon, England: Shearsman Books, 1984

The Club Fits Either Hand
New Rochelle, NY: Elizabeth Press, 1979

Both Hands Screaming
New Rochelle, NY: Elizabeth Press, 1975

Hands You Are Secretly Wearing
New Rochelle, NY: Elizabeth Press, 1972

Which Hand Holds the Brother: Poems, 1966 – 68
New Rochelle, NY: Elizabeth Press, 1969

Twenty Years of Hands
New Rochelle, NY: Elizabeth Press, 1966

I Counted Only April: First Poems
New Rochelle, NY: Elizabeth Press, 1964

The B Poems

Simon Perchik

POETS WEAR PRADA • Hoboken, New Jersey

The B Poems

Copyright © 2016 Simon Perchik

All rights reserved. Except for use in any review or for educational purposes, the reproduction or utilization of this work in whole or in part in any form by electronic, mechanical or other means, now known or hereafter invented, including xerography, photocopying and recording, or in any informational or retrieval system, is forbidden without the written permission of the publisher:

> Poets Wear Prada
> 533 Bloomfield Street, Second Floor
> Hoboken, New Jersey 07030
> http://pwpbooks.blogspot.com

First North American Publication 2016
First Mass Market Paperback Edition 2016

Grateful acknowledgment is made to the many publications where these poems, some in earlier versions, previously appeared. For a complete list of publication credits, please see the Acknowledgments.

ISBN-13: 978-0692450697
ISBN-10: 0692450696

Library of Congress Control Number: 2015941372

Printed in the U.S.A.

Front Cover Image: Jack Cooper
Author Photo: Rossetti Perchik

For Mickie

Table of Contents

B1	It never begins, you	3
B2	And the gust that circles these graves	4
B3	Just below the surface one arm	5
B4	Together with your knees	6
B5	As if this dirt can't overflow	7
B6	And the earth leans against you	8
B7	This shadow half iron, half	9
B8	You wash this floor the way winter	10
B9	The rain climbing along your wrist	11
B10	You must enjoy the risk	12
B11	You mourn the way this sand	13
B12	You have this kinship, the limp	14
B13	The dead the snow hold back	15
B14	One hand held out — you expect	18
B15	What a strange crop :the smell	17
B16	From the same glass	18
B17	These waves still surface, not sure	19
B18	This wall and sunlight	20
B19	Between these graves and every Sunday	21
B20	You come by though the hole	22
B21	Row after row	23
B22	Mouth to mouth this rock	24
B23	Already weightless these steps	26
B24	With its feeble hold this hillside	27
B25	From habit, burnt	28
B26	Its arms still around her, this dirt	29
B27	It's coal you're after, the part	30

B28	You reach for this facecloth	31
B29	Its ink is heavier at night	32
B30	This door half flowers	33
B31	Your fingers depend on somewhere far	34
B32	Finished — no new graves	35
B33	Before she got the chance! this canvas	36
B34	This rock no longer tries	37
B35	This cup grows nothing	38
B36	With your mouth closed	39
B37	Breaking apart :this calendar	40
B38	You begin the way shorelines	41
B39	These bricks reheated	42
B40	Slowly you have forgotten how	43
B41	Every wall has a resting place	44
B42	This fire escape once outside	45
B43	This rain has no moisture left, falls	46
B44	Unless this knob, as usual	48
B45	Still uneven, this dirt	49
B46	For a split-second these steps	50
B47	You tell this ice the glass	51
B48	You will hide, try	52
B49	You sprinkle the dead, closer than usual	53
B50	And though the dirt never dries	54
B51	Without a grammar	55
B52	To coax this rake you dig	56
B53	This stone has no shadow yet	57

B54	All that's left from the map	58
B55	The moon behind the moon	59
B56	These fences, half done, half	60
B57	You wait as if every river	61
B58	You can tell by the heat	62
B59	You can still make out the stars	63
B60	The dead are already holding hands	64
B61	Though the flash has left his hair	65
B62	Empty and the sand	66
B63	All day and your arms	67
Acknowledgments		68
About the Author		70

The B Poems

B1

It never begins, you
carry off this rain
not yet dry enough to be afraid

— there's no sky either
just your reaching down
and for the hundred hundredth time

this tombstone is still sharp
though what you touch
is too wide, stays soft

and what falls through
still sifts for dirt
that won't come closer

is already bleeding
and in your heart
as sand and thirst.

B2

And the gust that circles these graves
— they wander off, sweeping away
everything except the dirt

by now night after night
herded as small stones
though it's no longer raining

— what takes you by the hand
is this mud-caked headwind
holding you back so nothing dries

looks just for your lips
taken one beside the other
from your face and later.

B3

Just below the surface one arm
loosens in front the other
the way rock still breaks apart

for air — this bench leaks
needs nails and the wobble
full blown, half-beaten into it

half by your lips growing here
as grass that never strikes bottom
— kisses! needs cheeks to lock

when they come close and drown
— wood is useless now
though you count backwards

lifting the bench, empty it
on the ground that longs for you
and one bare hand as its own.

B4

Together with your knees
already half hands
— even the sky is lessened

lets this rain speak for two
the way stars leave you
— you come too close

and though you whisper
the dirt collapses, cools
till no one can escape

— just darkness
and the distance
that is not rain, that clings

tightens, makes from your voice
each cry smaller and smaller
back into your arms.

B5

As if this dirt can't overflow
has nothing behind it
except your fingertips
farther and farther apart

— you look for the waterline
the way each morning dries
closing in on you, half crater
half while this clay jar

begins to drink again
with its mouth and the flower
at home with you, here and there
covers you and nothing between.

B6

And the earth leans against you
from inside, starts its turn
hand over hand — you empty each box

slowly, smoothing the sides
then once it's dark
begin to dig for air

and wait for the corner
half cardboard, half taking you in
and no one home though here you are

opening a door the way every star
smells from dying winds and grass
— you unpack, thinner and thinner

as if the air is losing heart
bending its climb and doors
no longer by the hundreds.

B7

This shadow half iron, half
reaching out, breaking loose
— with both hands the hands

that no longer come for you
and in their place the dirt
grows back together

— in such a wound you die
in two places at the same time
make a path for the sky

you remember and underneath
— nothing but your arms
tearing each other apart

— handful by handful there's room
for a little more shadow
a little more you can say.

B8

You wash this floor the way winter
waits for its ice to stir
show more interest in coming closer

and the drowned — what bubbles up
is bottom sand though you drift
and farther out more water

unable to dry so far from home
— a single drop by drop
wipes down the world and longing

— it's how you sleep
leaking from your pores
this side then that breaking open

holding on to each other and now
without shape, making it through
as surfaces and nearer.

B9

The rain climbing along your wrist
makes it seem easy — you breathe
through your hand, for two

— it helps to wet your eyelids
look where water has taken root
in pieces, knows how to grieve

the way your arm throws out
its still warm breezes and each morning
heavier — dirt learned this long ago

still fills your mouth with the word
for sister so nothing
can break without thirst

or blossom or with your hand
crushing you for more tears
and morning after morning.

Bio

You must enjoy the risk
swallowing rainwater, splashing
so close to the ground

wait alone for the train
you know is never in time
can't rub the tracks dry

or keep you from leaning too far
— it's the chance you take, wave
— sometimes waves, sometimes for nothing.

B 11

You mourn the way this sand
has no strength, keeps warm
between one day and another

and your closed hands
that need the place
left by a small stone

dropping slowly in water
though what rests here
is the emptiness already mist

and nothing starts again
— you dig as if this beach
blossoms once your fingers

open and these dead
lose their way among the flowers
that no longer come home

— you kneel easily now
pulled down by your shadow
following head first as rain

heavier and heavier
tracing a face with just your lips
and worn-out nod.

B12

You have this kinship, the limp
balances you and the earth
already blossoming

with nothing under it
though you lift one foot
closer to the other

hillside after hillside
the way mud settles and clots
— you're used to losing, come

so this cane can grab your hand
almost in time and what's left
above the ground, knows

you're drowning, in rain
stops and starts, in dirt
and tells you everything.

B13

The dead the snow holds back
you rub between your hands
— it's glare you're after

before it disappears
the way a cemetery fence
is painted, then overflows

— to get more white
you let this bathroom sink
open up in water

wrap the soap over and over
in that same wood
still burning — how else

can you bathe, the door
closed then following you out
chased by flowers and the cold.

B14

One hand held out — you expect
it to end pressed against a rain
already mixed with turns

and falling too far
— what you will remember
is how this road died down

though you needed both hands
when it counted
the way these handlebars

still reach for a quiet place
and the sound your arms make
when holding close — she

would forget with you
what's ahead, sometimes
dripping, sometimes she would lean

as far as possible
without touching your bones
or make room.

B15

What a strange crop :the smell
spread out the way this mud is plowed
already warmed by the descent

used to one, one more, one more
though you are circling it
with your mouth left open

holding nothing, moving nothing
nothing but this dirt
no longer thirsty, confident

— what struggles here is the rain
still on the ground, thinning out
as lakes, at most as lips and distances

— here you've got to bend
to get a closer grip, pull up
this hillside broken loose

and lean into where this water takes you
handcuffed, smashed against the rocks
and on your knees more kisses.

B16

From the same glass
— it's the risk they take
jumpy, out in the open

the way a puddle, to this day
ices over, survives the winter
as one hand uneasy with another

— you drink from a glass
too heavy, half frost, half
water that keeps its voice

safe, no longer in some stream
listening for more water
though you drown holding on

to your favorite glass
that no longer remembers you
or better days.

B17

These waves still surface, not sure
it's her lips that open and close, kept moist
though you can't hear her voice

scented with rotting wood, weeds
and bottom sand — you row this boat
left, right, swinging your arms

half moonlight, half almost makes out
the words rising from empty shells
and the dress you first saw her in

— you need more arms, clear summer nights
from that inch-by-inch love song
heavier than these overgrown paths

no longer listening for her forehead
that once anchored the earth
and water too knows what it has

reeling from a gentle stroke, another
another, facing the sky
it leaves behind, caressing her hair

her breasts, her shimmering — some nights
you can hear her, one by one
— some nights it's colder, colder.

B18

This wall and sunlight
hiding under the faded wallpaper
though its flowers no longer move

— a single 3X5 snapshot
brings the room down
in flames and farther off

the rickety wooden frame
smelling from corners
already broken open

lifted alongside in pieces
and the glass in pieces
holds you closer, closer

and your chest keeps warm
— it alone left standing
as if the wall you don't use anymore

could recognize the place
without getting lost, or your voice
or the arms next to her.

B19

Between these graves and every Sunday
you bring the wide, floppy hat
— on each visit, the red scarf

before the light she asks for
cools, hardens into the back and forth
that cradles each small stone

— she's not interested in stone
and tells you so though it's not Sunday
— it's not any day, just winter

stone bars and you wait outside
for the gate to show up
or how long she's been in.

B20

You come by though the hole
has no other place to go
waits behind this ice-packed dirt

left over from when the sun
had no choice either, spreading out
as emptiness, the last resort

— this hole must sense it will die
the way the sun died, was buried
in the open, alone, circling down

strangely quiet with nothing to cling to
except the endless under and under
just to reach winter, to lift

and care for it — you visit the left out
built from years and years
but you are asking the impossible

with just your fingers — on tiptoe
would make it easier, anything
would make it easier.

B21

Row after row
— it's your usual vineyard
overrun the way mourners

will always lean too far
are already in clusters
holding on to a stone

as if a sharper knife
could fall through
and deep inside each vine

leave no one to walk past
though you come for work
with wobbling fingers

that no longer make you sad
— you pluck each pebble
trying not to touch the dead

show up as if they
would never let you leave
with nothing in your mouth

except as some seedling
just planted and on your lips
the dirt is somehow sweeter

growing itself into arms
and legs and kisses, by now
even in winter the stars.

B22

Mouth to mouth this rock
takes back that light
the sun grew fat on

though birds gag in it
still part their wings
not yet the ashes

that run through you
let their last breath
reach under you, hold on

till nothing's left
except the shadow
the dirt counts on

— you don't dig anymore
afraid more darkness
will escape, unfold

as in midair
the slow wide climbing turn
into mountainside

unaware how long it's been
— you sift, lean over
the way this tiny rock

is pulling you closer
wingtip to wingtip
is swallowing you

as if one by one
its feathers had opened
— in time, in time.

B23

Already weightless these steps
don't need the morning
back away as that emptiness

stars are used to
— you can hear them narrowing
creaking and from behind

wait for the sun to open fire
flash past your forehead
though you can't make out

the week or year or the cloud
that knows you're there
comes for you between more rain

and mountainside still standing
no longer growing grass
can't love or remember

— you hide the way this attic
opens inside a door
that is not a flower

— an iron knob
that turns away nothing
and in your arms nothing, nothing.

B24

With its feeble hold this hillside
— a simple bond though your shadow
is pulling loose — this dirt

won't keep its promise
as if nearness means nothing
even when you expect the sun

handful by handful, back
to warm itself
yet you still come here alone

can almost make out the breasts
the eyebrows and on this mound
the forehead you long for, the eyes

that rise from this leftover darkness
as two mornings and at night
two nights, closer and closer.

B25

From habit, burnt
as if every morning now
the sun has to be reheated

still frightened by the cold
more than coming alone
— it's your usual meal

two slices, made stale
broken open the way coffee
just by boiling

turns your mouth black
— you've learned to open bread
till it reeks with ashes

and smoke already rising
to become another mouth
and on its lips

the small blister, resting
though there's no moon
only this side by side

lowered slowly, no longer
empty, your arms cramped
calling for each other.

B26

Its arms still around her, this dirt
clings between what's left behind
and the rain — its stones stare back

can't make out the fingers nearby
easily yours and with each handful
something that is not her forehead

just the over-and-over nearness
you pull closer and with your mouth
welcomes this dirt, covers it

the way any helpless wound is kept moist
and on her cheeks, something later
no longer remembers, barely dry.

B27

It's coal you're after, the part
that burns the way evenings
still grieve in place

— you count on it to heat these dead
though in that darkness
half nightfall, half

no longer warm, came
to a standstill
already rolled into one

shaped by the split-second
that opens all stone, stays
forever in its pieces

— you collect promises :rocks
owe you something
will break apart, take hold

as the whispers they once were
though black is the something
that's extra, that delivers

regroups and even in sunlight
touches your cheek, unsure
helps you remember.

B28

You reach for this facecloth
the way every bridge is built
reminds the dead — sway

though water is older than sunlight
older than rain and wave after wave
— you have so many mouths, drink

from a rag carried across
as shoreline and someone's death
— so much cloth, clinging to water

that waits for its darkness
for your touch, breathless
in secret, tighter and tighter.

B29

Its ink is heavier at night
though you can still hear the hum
from some sea already faint
when sunlight too was black
lost, floated lifeless

— you still write to her
piecing word to far-off word
till their darkness escapes
sleepless, so close to your arms

— a single wave pulls the others in
brings down each page before it dries
into dirt and forgetting
lowers one evening more
that will weigh too much.

B30

This door half flowers
half wood in back some horse
dripping with saliva
wishes it was born dead

— the knob won't turn
though the sun's nearby
exhausted, wobbles
the way even light
withers, reaches an end
limps till the room
fits between your jaws

— they never let go
still drink from a bowl
that doesn't move anymore
bends open for dirt
as if you had no thirst
no arms left or side to side.

B31

Your fingers depend on somewhere far
no longer boiling as sunlight
— they huddle the way the mad

are cured, splashed in a mist
half ice, half crushed between
the first caress and darkness

— they make a fist, cling
as if counting backwards this dirt
would point in a straight line

though what will become the sun
is not warm yet — inches old
already spreading out in need.

B32

Finished — no new graves
though yesterday you counted boats
— side by side, adrift

breaking apart under the rocks
— done! here you are
adding rafts to the way

each sea long ago learned
how deep inside the storm
there must be a very big number

— a half-finished arithmetic
where you can't carry over by one
the hand so close to the other

pulling on weeds
so you can include your fingers
take hold as if these dead

would never let go
and their great weight, their place
waiting in line.

B33

Before she got the chance! this canvas
fitted to a wooden frame though her hair
is hid by fragrant oils and waves, the comb

not yet bone — it's enough
a damp brush will shape it
over and over the way every mask

has the scent you expect from graves
— the artist tried, wiped her forehead
with a shadow that is not dirt

lets her disappear unfinished
and the drought already winter
clings to this wall and lower.

B34

This rock no longer tries
though you give each grave
the tool it needs

— does it matter
you haven't looked here in years
— you bring the dead

and your forehead each day
closer to the ground
easy to grab, hold close

let it harden, already
scraped for the powder
that cures, can stop the breathing.

B35

This cup grows nothing
and though you add more water
it boils away, half

tighter and tighter, half
wants you to get some sleep
has become your darling

found a home for your lips
used to fever, smoke
and the slow climbing turn

that stays moist
waits for the rim to cling
left open and shaking.

B36

With your mouth closed
swallow though this rain
is already rain and further on

— you have a taste for darkness
fill your belly the way the earth
each night escapes as a small hole

clings to one hillside
carried by another — you become
its grave, eat without fingers

without knees or the headlong dive
this dirt is used to, held down
and looking for more rain

for shoreline starting out
not yet a whisper, lost
cleared away and for your lips.

B37

Breaking apart :this calendar
half as if memory, half
still exploding though the paint

reeks from weather vanes
and rain, last seen
mixed with snow

— without your glasses
you can't make out if the wind
will dry in time

and a second coat already warms
the way you keep track
by lifting rugs, tables, chairs

— you need the pieces :lids
that will flare up
shake off their cracks

with each brush then back
till nothing ages
even with the window open.

B38

You begin the way shorelines
risk their life this close
though after each funeral

you drown in the row by row
where each photograph is overturned
shaken loose from the family album

— her shoes seem pleased
to be shoes, not walk anymore
or store their darkness for later

— the family was always collecting
wanted you to sit, not pose barefoot
but there you are, even now

standing next to her, eye to eye
without saying a word, would leave
if you knew how to turn away

the blank page, solid black
not a beach, not a breath, nothing
that understands this emptiness.

B39

These bricks reheated
remember circling up
sifting the smoke

for smoke not yet stars
still inside, terrified
by its darkness — chimneys

know to focus the sky closer
as the night that comes due
blackens this hillside

already in place
brought down from under
no longer red — they aim

the way each shadow
leans against your heart
tries to warm itself

in grasses and your hands
made bigger, so slowly
nothing can save you.

B40

Slowly you have forgotten how
and after each rain reach out
as if this folding ladder

once skimmed the rooftops
was taught to trust the sky
though rung by rung

you no longer lead the dead
to the dead trapped above you
and what passes for rescue

never leaves the ground
or backs away, shaky, not sure
what headwinds do or don't

— you have forgotten how to fly
want to be lifted, lifted again
as seasons and afterward

and hand over hand return
with the blue-gray flight path
covered with dirt and later.

B41

Every wall has a resting place
kept warm though in the dark
it drains, overgrown with cracks

and grasses :you brush on footpaths
the way every greenhouse is nourished
heated by the mouth on your mouth

— another coat seems reasonable
so you paint this wall over and over
till what's left standing overflows

never dries into that slow love song
from before the sun grew huge
it would fit into this room, had time

to stay and night not yet surrounded
falling behind, from far away
weeping into nothing at all.

B42

This fire escape once outside
already knows the risk
yet it's the tenement

abandoned, clinging to a street
fallen to its death
as sunlight, still in the open

— the sun is not enough
two are needed, they calm
each other and side by side

— two suns! mouth to mouth
the way all wings open
wave to the dead

even with your eyes closed
the morning larger than usual
the fire that is your home.

B43

This rain has no moisture left, falls
as the light from bells
struck from behind

the way all hillsides
are hollowed out for stars
no brighter than this grass

though these graves never know
where next, they listen
for pieces, reminded

by how the first sun
broke apart — they hear it
in the dried-up warmth

for which your shadow is made
— what they hear
no longer remembers

your heart was where
it was safe
and before your heart

waves that started its cry
toward the second sun
and then another, then another

and yet this rain comes back
even without a sky
comes as in the beginning

in splendor, not yet a morning
on the over-and-over thirst
still not allowed in the open.

B44

Unless this knob, as usual
swollen the way each star
still has to be pulled sideways

— what makes the door shriek
is just its darkness reaching out
for crumbs, hungry, terrified

— for a long time now
these hinges haven't worked
clogged by your hand

turning on the light
to tell from where it falls
the year, the month :the sides

closing in — night after night
and once alongside
they forget how dark it was

force the door to stay awake
count from the beginning
and over your shoulders.

B45

Still uneven, this dirt
was built from leftovers
that never dry, smoothed

then fills your chest
with salt, used again
as shoreline and thirst

though you lower your lips
for the finishing touch
not yet swallowed in anger

— what you bury is the earth
this time in pieces, unsure
where the mouth goes

once made into a rain
already dust
that doesn't bother anymore.

B46

For a split-second these steps
are at a loss, half thorns
half holding back just enough

in case you come too close
and your shadow no longer means
you still face the sun

the way this stairway will dissolve
as rainwater, would close your eyes
if there was time

— where you wade is already wood
smoothed by the same descent
streams are famous for

can tell from a single stone
on the bottom for years
following under footmarks then flowers

that stay open alongside the others
till suddenly you are ankle-deep
breathing out again, there.

B47

You tell this ice the glass
is breaking up, to take
one breath more :a splash

starting out, half as shoreline
the other frozen underneath
so you don't drown the way each shadow

still has the scent from seawater
though the frost
is already holding your hand

face down, deeper and deeper
in pieces not yet apart
— you yell, breathe in, let its cold

wash over you, in you, become
water again, a mouth again
and against your lips, alone.

B48

You will hide, try
point to your forehead
almost remember where the mourners

put the dirt back
so even you won't know the difference
— you need more dirt :a sky

with one cloud then another
filled with stones and gasping for air
so you will think it's the grasses

that have forgotten where to go
have nothing left to do
the way funerals still come by

as if rain no longer mattered at night
and the kiss someone once gave you
— you won't eat anymore :the breeze

will step back, go slack, cover you
though there's not enough room
with distances and longing.

B49

You sprinkle the dead, closer than usual
as if something inside this rock
is just now learning to survive

without roots, already talks
about lying awake, afraid your fingers
will crack it open for the mouth

to cover the one that's started
the way night over night your hands
spread out as the distance

that empties only into river water
so it comes up each morning
held in place, not yet breathing.

B50

And though the dirt never dries
a simple circle makes it easy
— your fingertip begins to warm

then later the emptiness
it's used to — by heart
curves in as if the grass

knows nothing about the tiny waves
leaving shore alone and the old life
already around your shoulders

— the dead never expected your lips
so close, on the bottom
will never know what they wanted.

B51

Without a grammar
you practice the handshake
sure whatever comes by

can be reasoned with
let you pump this dirt out
till its word for sister

is no longer bitter
and handful by handful
empty your mouth

already alongside
and face to face
nothing you say matters.

B52

To coax this rake you dig
a nest, your shoulder
already growing feathers

weighs almost nothing
and more than anyplace else
its shadow flutters, lowers

along the branches :the sun
must sense how huge it is
and these leaves everywhere

have begun to carry back
its mornings, making room
as handful by handful

the way each hole circles down
to begin again, fills
with winter then with distances.

B53

This stone has no shadow yet
though it turns to you
as if the dirt no longer keeps it warm

— this small it needs to be held
is learning to cry in the open
no older than this morning

covered with frost and side by side
— it clings to you, watches the dead
make room for it and between their arms

become the sun whose pieces
are now your heart, part lost
part falling back, these.

B54

All that's left from the map
is this birdbath — you can't make out
the north, northeast or if the wind

is in the same place, skimming
lower and lower as shoreline
not sure you're still there

or did the water dry by itself
— you rely on it, need this landmark
to locate exactly where

and you make the sharp turn
deep into birdsong and the cries
that follow behind, end over end

with both hands and the ground
spills out its air, there's room
for you and in all directions.

B55

The moon behind the moon
works its huge tides
the way you rotate this switch

and the wall still warm
dims, struggles to hold on
as the silt and afterglow

you use for coastline :a mouth
where the knob stops
condemned to circle back

— without thinking! you peel
and slowly a great darkness
drifts over you, whispers

though it is already hiding
another shadow, pulling it
closer, still weak, has her forehead.

B56

These fences, half done, half
still counting the afternoons
that return alone and those

with no way out — the dead
must like it here, come by
bring the family, lawns, let you

get to know the neighbors
birthdays, what they remember
— this colony has built its city

on staves broken off as sunlight
that looks away though the gate
is open, used to your shadow

spreading out to cool, holding off
step by step where the name goes
when you give it back and in shame.

B57

You wait as if every river
begins in ice, then moonlight
seeping slowly through

— you don't wait! the coffee
is sweeping all Earth
on its side, both poles

flowing into the equator
and what you swallow
is already shoreline

huddled around this table
and your lips in the open
the way small stones are left

to help the dead wander back
as the dim light they make
and any morning now.

B58

You can tell by the heat
though they long ago gave up
the search for water and air

and with every death another
comes to this dry riverbed
already hillside, warmed

by some invisible spore
deep inside and your hands
around it, closed

the way each footpath slows
still gathering the others
who take too long in the curve

— all these rocks! and the dirt
peels off till what you hear
is everywhere the sun

not yet born and in your arms
bit by bit broken apart
with care and mornings.

B59

You can still make out the stars
though it's noon and the beach
changes — you can tell by the feel

and listening for engine scrap
breaking apart, smelling from smoke
expects you to stand up barefoot

keep struggling with shoreline
— you're not new to this
will start the grill weeks ahead

as if stars are never sure
are milling around, forgot all about
the darkness you're breathing in

and no way now to pick and choose
the fires however small or close
to some ocean or daylight

till it creaks and your mouth
no longer lit for kisses
and songs about nothing.

B60

The dead are already holding hands
and what's left they share
as memories — in the meantime

who do you suppose makes this tea
and the smoked fish, then room
for the grandchildren you almost forgot

were born later — the dead
are no better at it than you
— they mix up dates and places

though what pins them down
is no longer the flowers
soothed by each other and vague streams

— no, it wasn't you lifting this cup
passing itself off as empty
with nothing inside to unwrap

— from the start the dead form a circle
as if they still expect to sing out loud
and you would hear it, open your mouth.

B61

Though the flash has left his hair
combed back with hers held down
by iron straps and waiting — the dead

are never ready for a wedding
go house to house, ask for enough
in case you've seen these two

alive somewhere, rubbing their eyes
as if the photographer might set off
another miracle and nothing change

the way every grave goes door to door
as rain — would jam each drop open
alongside all these flowers, smelling

from bare wire, fresh dirt, storms
counting the ones that already
reached the ground and not moving.

B62

Empty and the sand
follows you along Broadway
as if some dampness

was left for shoreline
moves the IRT up
then down the way clammers

use their feet to rake
— you walk on tracks
careful not to miss

while the train underneath
breaks open its doors
all at once — no, you don't jump

nothing like that
— these shells are the same
the mad feel for

though their sweat takes the place
water grieves into
and their mouths are the same

let you yell down
and not a mark inside your body
to call you by.

B63

All day and your arms
need the smock loose
and white gloves

— this barnacle is the kind
that spirals toward the light
already nurses

on a rock half at anchor
half this kitchen table
— a small loaf and already

ravenous though once it's cut
it begins to circle closer
and what your arms free

is no longer joined at the heart
born over and over
as twins facing each other

lets you see your own lips
and in the darkness
that belongs to you both.

Acknowledgments

This author extends his thanks to the editors of the following magazines in which these poems, some in earlier versions, previously appeared: *Abramelin*; *Abraxes*; *Abridged*; *Alembic*; *Amoskeag*; *Apocryphaltext*; *Arnazella*; *Art:Mag*; *Aurorean*; *Bacon*; *Bakery*; *Barnwood*; *Beatlick News*; *Beloit*; *Blue Collar*; *Briar Cliff*; *Burnside*; *Burnt District*; *Caliban*; *Chaffin Journal*; *Challenger International*; *Chiron*; *Common Ground*; *Comstock*; *Conceit*; *Concho River*; *Controlled Burn*; *Counterexample Poetics*; *Cream City*; *Cresset*; *Denver Quarterly*; *Deronda*; *Dos Passos*; *Edgz*; *Ekphrasis*; *Euphony*; *Eureka*; *Fluent Ascension*; *Fogged Clarity*; *Former People Journal*; *Four Ties*; *Freshwater*; *Fugue*; *Futures Trading*; *Gihon River*; *Grab-a-Nickel*; *Green Hills Literary Lantern*; *Hamilton Stone*; *Hanging Loose*; *Heeltap*; *Home Planet News*; *Homestead*; *Hurricane*; *Icon*; *Illumen*; *Indiana*; *Interim*; *Iowa*; *Istanbul Literary*; *J Journal*; *The Journal*; *Kaimana*; *Kerf*; *Laurel*; *Licking River*; *Lone Start*; *Mad Hatter's*; *Mandala Journal*; *Marco Polo*; *Milo*; *Möbius, The Poetry Magazine*; *Moon*; *Mouse Tales*; *Narrow Fellow*; *New Letters*; *New Plains*; *New Review of Literature*; *North American*; *Northeast*; *Oasis*; *Off Course*; *Off the Coast*; *On the Rusk*; *Osiris*; *Otis Nebula*; *Parting Gifts*; *Paterson Literary*; *Pembroke*; *Philadelphia Poets*; *Phoebe*; *Pilgrimage Magazine*; *Plain Brown Wrapper*; *Plainsongs*; *Poesia*; *Poetry Depth Quarterly*; *PoetsWest*; *Portland*; *Prairie Schooner*; *Prairie Winds*; *Presa*; *Pretty Owl*; *Prick of the Spindle*; *Pudding Magazine*; *Puritan Magazine*; *Raven*; *Red Booth*; *Review Americana*; *River Poets Journal*; *Rockhurst*; *Rust+Moth*; *San Pedro River*; *Sassafras Magazine*; *Selzer*; *Sentinel Quarterly*; *Shampoo*; *Spare Change*; *Stand*; *Stillwater*; *Storm Cellar*; *Stride*; *This Great Society*; *Thrush*; *Transcendent Visions*; *Turk's Head Review*; *Utter Magazine*; *Verse*; *Visions*; *Whirlwind*; *Wilderness House*; *Works & Days*; *Write This*; *Zombie Logic*; *Zymbol*; and *ZYX*.

I further acknowledge my debt to James L. Weil, Edward Butscher, and Anselm Parlatore for their poetry and friendship; to Deborah Light for the generous access to her voluminous collection of myths; to the owners, employees, and customers of both Fierro's Pizzeria and The Golden Pear where these poems were written.

Finally, the 63 poems in this collection would not exist had it not been for the 63 photographs in Bruce Davidson's 1990 *Photofile* to inspire and guide their composition (*Bruce Davidson: Photofile*, London: Thames & Hudson, 1990), nor for pivotal articles that appeared in *Science News Magazine*.

About the Author

Attorney for many years, poet many more, Simon Perchik brings coincidence to the turn of a page. His father, a silk weaver prior to the Great Depression, that instar of American twentieth-century life, when mills, satanic and otherwise, succumbed to the dark (thenceforth a grocer), framed texture shimmering with light through layers of hidden, prismatic fiber. Son, too, would stand by circumstance as condition required: born Jewish on Christmas Eve 1923. Yossarian view during World War II vouchsafed glimpse of an abstract high above, far exceeding the avant-garde. A walk one day after the war brought him face to façade with an impressive edifice he had paused to admire. This proved to be NYU, *then*, coinciding with the G.I. Bill, foreword to studying Law.

Coincidence implies concinnity of unlikely and unlike. Opposites, reconciled through partial interpolation of jurisprudence, prosodically extrapolated to serve the notion of metaphor, discommode predilection toward received idea. Absent constraint of expectation, off the manifold path encircling cliché, leading past syntax and around semantics, guided only by vatic susceptibility to nuance and the dissonance of the irrational sufficient to allay anguish and achieve release, the poet — reader, often posed on his or her back — pursues simile amid anomalies of adventitious image and personal interpretation. Since inspiration first drawn from a sort of phosphorescence, imagination has largely been lit by the interior.

Simon's is a studio art, disjoined from the actual world, even words. An impartial genesis *uncovered* through chance, initiated with photographs, his method elicits a subjective independence and tendency for words to align, associate, suggest, and contend with inverse occurrence. Simon assembles the diverse emblems and disparate elements of this will, weaves them in fine. Elusive to the eye, less spoken than seemed imagined aloud, as memory evinces thought, a limpidity nevertheless oversees its design, a vernacular precision, concise as the painter's brush, transcends understanding what cannot be articulated. Everything rises to the surface at once, a universe portrayed in which *best* exceeds *all* end of knowledge, ordinary conjoins extraordinary, unconscious of poet and reader become one.

A NOTE ON THE TYPE

To furnish titles for *The B Poems*, Papyrus pairs fantasy with the unfeasible. Ranging beyond even the so-called old style typefaces inspired by scribal diligence, it imagines a language that does not exist yet (English) rendered on a surface contemporary two millennia preceding its design in 1982. Hand-drawn, combining calligraphic pen and textured paper, by Chris Costello — playing bass and electric guitar — rough edges, irregular curves, and high horizontal strokes distinguishing its capitals convey the fibrous striations of actual pith, commended to display. Released by Letraset in 1983, packaged by Microsoft and Mac, and reputedly far too popular for its own good (should such be possible), it appeals, particularly, where a touch of the antique, even ancient if not ancient and future, is desired, as, for instance, the movie *Avatar*, church bulletins, and coffee shops; the last, here suitable, because Simon Perchik's favored place of composition.

Typography recapitulates the struggle between the *poetic* and reality. The technology that implements it must contend with surfaces that not only vary but alter the method of its presentation. Text in *The B Poems* is set in Constantia, a serif typeface doubly *transitional* — in the earliest sense of styling different (or Baroque) from the first metal Renaissance designs, and by intended use for imaging on screen in addition to the printed page.

Versatility balances simultaneous appeal to the eye of the reader and the connoisseur looking beyond legibility to the aesthetic. Designed by John Hudson, a multilingual specialist in the depiction of scripts ancient, exotic, and arcane (Ogham, Sinhalese, and Cherokee, for example), Constantia achieves benchmark fluency for continuous text, the lingua franca of contract lawyers. One of six typefaces created in conjunction with Microsoft's ClearType text-rendering technology (and the initial letter "C"), Constantia, released in 1983, takes its name from Latin, meaning "constancy." At odds with company lawyers whose fear of trademark infringement continued to narrow the choices of possible nomenclature, Hudson, one evening, singing psalms during vespers, heard "constantia" intoned. He later confessed that the sight of seabirds had made him regret that he hadn't chosen to call the typeface Cormorant.

www.ingramcontent.com/pod-product-compliance
Lightning Source LLC
Chambersburg PA
CBHW031208090426
42736CB00009B/829